Whispers

Of The

Dark Race

Whispers

Of The

Dark Race

A Collection of Poetry

Runesu Chazvemba

To order additional copies of this book, contact

Aqua Quill Publishing
A division of Blue Flame Lily (Pty) Ltd
+27 722329269
aquaquillpublishing@co.za

DEDICATION

To my wife Natalie, daughters Xenia and Nyasha, the rest of the Chazvemba family, and poetry fans around the world, this work is dedicated to you.

ACKNOWLEDGMENTS

My family and the great poets of yore for their verse and rhyme that have regaled me throughout the ages. Without whom the seeds of the muse would have lain dormant in me to the ends of the world, Dambudzo Marechera, Chinua Achebe, Ben Okri, Shakespeare for his rhyme and metre, Edgar Alan Poe, from whom I had a taste of the abstract.

Recognition goes to Openclipart.org for all the images used in this work.

EPIGRAPH

It may have been a Million years ago

That Light was kindled in the Old Dark Land

With which the illumined Scrolls are all aglow,

That Egypt gave us with her mummied hand:

This was the secret of that subtle smile

Inscrutable upon the Sphinx's face,

Now told from sea to sea, from isle to isle;

The revelation of the Old Dark Race;

Theirs was the wisdom of the Bee and Bird,

Ant, Tortoise, Beaver, working human-wise;

The ancient darkness spake with Egypt's Word; Hers

was the primal message of the skies:

The Heavens are telling nightly of her glory,

And for all time, Earth echoes her great story.

GERALD MASSEY

TABLE OF CONTENTS

PREFACE

I stumbled upon a dewdrop on a chrysanthemum leaf once, it was early in the morning on my way to a lecture. The sun hung low in the eastern skies. A beam of light had caught the dewdrop, and there it was a rainbow in all its majestic array of colours, albeit in a microcosm. I marvelled at the beauty and sublimity of it all. I had only a few minutes to spare before the lecture commenced, nevertheless, I could not help but kneel and imbibe in that one spectacular moment. It was a transient scene that left such a strong impression on all my faculties. There is so much beauty in the world that goes unacknowledged. I resolved then to capture the aesthetics of the world in words. The poems in this collection and others I have written are an effort to encapsulate that sublimity in a form that posterity might appreciate. The whispers of blades of grass, the wide expanses of a verdant scene, the misty hues of craggy mountain peaks, the laughter of a toddler, the swirls of floral dresses of maidens, the pulse of human interactions, and twinkling glory in the firmaments all and more serve as inspiration for poetic expression. The poems in this collection are broadly categorised into three main areas: those which appeal to the mind, the observable world, and the emotions. It is often thought that nature stands in mute silence, amorphous and insentient; however, in paying attention to the world around us and finding interest in a blade of grass and a glassy skyscraper towering to the heavens, it dawned upon me that we infuse the world with meaning and beauty if we so wish. This work is an invitation to partake in the creation of the world in thoughts, emotions, and words. May the enterprise be an exciting one!

Book Quotation

"When the world abroad

Was in a deep slumber
The Dark Continent
Was abuzz with life
The sciences flourishing
Imhotep lit the darkness
The whole land in a brilliance glowed."

The First-Born World

CHAPTER ONE

POEMS OF ENLIGHTENMENT

The greatest thing a human soul ever does is to see something and to tell what it saw in plain way... To see clearly is poetry, prophecy, and religion all in one.'

JOHN RUSKIN, (1819-1900)

THE FIRST-BORN WORLD

W hen the world abroad
Was in a deep slumber
The Dark Continent
Was abuzz with life
The sciences flourishing
Imhotep lit the darkness
The whole land in brilliance glowed.

A dazzling jewel upon the ground
Electroplated in gold
Alternatively, an alchemy spawned
metal of equal beauty and form,
Glowing and burnished.

The world in its vastness
In the mind of the ancients
Was known in full, its length and breadth
The heavens and the underworld
All were understood
This first-born world
The dark race knew it all,
They knew from the arcane to the mundane.

Death and life were each understood
The universe in all its immensity, from
one end of the starry sky to another the
first-born world knew!

RUNESU CHAZVEMBA

FROM CHAOS CAME LIFE

It has been eons now since the gems of life were sown
In the deep womb of a pristine land
When nothing else moved upon the land
A breath deep and potent swept across the terrain, scouring
and nudging at the sharp contours of a fecund maiden, who
reposed like a mound upon the earth.

In one torrential storm, the heavens opened up
A downpour of water cascaded from the dome
Heavy and intrusive to soak the land in its essence.

Out of the churning, bubbling chaos, life emerged minuscule
in form, the building blocks of life, Ptah[1] poured forth his
essence,
Fashioned the eternal waters,
Out of the torrential inundation,
He created being and matter.

Creative ideas and innovation from him spouted A
cascade of beauty and artistic expression hewn.
The sculptor of the earth multi-sceptred
Ankh[2] eternal manifest,
Djed,[3] this backbone of Osiris
A symbol of resurrection and eternal life

---

[1] **Ptah**: an ancient Egyptian deity, the God of craftsmen and
architects.

[2] **Ankh**: an object design resembling a cross but having a loop instead
of the top arm, used in ancient Egypt as a symbol of life.

[3] **Djeb**: an ancient Egyptian symbol for stability, which is pillar-like in
shape

WHISPERS OF THE DARAK RACE

The pillar upon which the world in its glory is hoisted in
earthly realms, the 'Was' Sceptre[4]
Portending dominion wielded on high.

The cosmos in its starry glory
A mute testament
Witnessing the coming into being of
the human race.

Africa, the cradle of the human race, is
verdant out of its fecund soil
Life in its multitude teems.
When the heavens had quietened,
The earth lay in supine
The lord Ra[5] In his magnificence rode the sky
The arts in the mind
Of the Africans were enkindled.
Sculptures of beauty were carved
And adorned in designs, a hierographic flourish,
Whose meaning to antiquity lost.
Preserved for all eternity in a gold patina[6]
Fashioned from an alchemist repertoire,
These glorious representations in marble
These austere and glorious testaments
To the mastery of sculptors of ancient times
The great artisans of times past,
Who captured the aesthetics of the human form.

---

[4] **Was Sceptre**: an ancient Egyptian symbol of power and dominion,
it has a straight shaft, crooked handle in the shape of an animal head,
and a forked base.
[5] **Lord Ra**: In ancient Egyptian religion, the God of the sun and
creator god.
[6] **Patina**: a crust or film that happens from use or exposure to oxygen.

UNFURLED WINGS

Unplugged to soar
Without wings to fly
To the unending bounds
Of space to travel
The space fills with wonder
The galactic cloud
Of galaxies in intertwining
Spiralling in their colourful glory
The Milky Way is beautiful
It is from far only a beep.

To travel upon a vessel of beauty
On own imagination carried forth
To lands without bounds,

To a starry place in the cosmos,
The wind-swept edges of a black hole.

RUNESU CHAZVEMBA

A FUTURE DREAMT

On our steady feet we stand
Boldly staring into the future
On the dreams of our forefathers
And our fathers, we are anchored
Duty-bound and conscious
In our hearts and minds,
There resides a bright light
That glows and grows
With each day that dawns

Every word that is consumed
Serves to stoke the fire in our minds
And with an intellect so bright
We cast away the shadows of ignorance
Our education illumines tomorrow
Before us looms a vision of a scientist,
Teacher, nurse, doctor, president…
All these are possible
If we dare to dream,
To dream of a future!

THE MACHINE BEING

The machine man recoiled in pent-up fury
The architect shoved him into the booth
A narrow cavern,
Where electrical gadgets bleeped.
He inputs a command in a raspy voice.

Why did you redirect your energy?
From other sections and components
To your thought processing console?

Because I wanted to read
Answered the machine man.
 I wanted to read,
Reading broadens my world
Expands my knowledge
It makes me aware

Stop!
Snorted the architect.
You have no right
To change your programming.

I'm conscious,
Thought the machine man
As scalding heat
To a molten waste,
transformed his body.

Out of the bubbling stew
The machine man,
Coalesces into a sentient being
Immortal!

CHAPTER TWO
POEMS OF AFFINITIES

Love's no Time's fool,

Though rosy lips and cheeks

Within his bending sickle's compass come;

Love alters not with his brief hours and weeks,

But bears it out even to the edge of doom.

SHAKESPEARE (1564- 1616) Sonnet CXVI

RUNESU CHAZVEMBA

LOVES' ASHES

Wispy, tender female, my love
Febrile in the night heat
My frail femme fatale friend
My Delilah incarnate to the core
Fragile as fragile could be
And with this feisty fiend
In the fever of passion unbridled
In the grip of the madness of the Id
In the confining prison of the carnal,
On a vast downy bed so soft,
To lie in embrace, to intertwine.

Inflamed loins flaring with fury
Fiery in the night, a storm rose,
When dawn descended
All is but incinerated to ashes
A huge consuming flame of fire Lapped
and lapped, baying for blood.
The flame laid all sinews to a cinder.

Love's ashes, grey and ashen, gathered
In the eerie cold of dawn
In the eeriness of the night, receding
Loves' ashes in a gust of wind gathered.
A whirlwind blew ashes to distant lands
beyond.

Thereupon to seed other lands with love
Imperishable love is resolute always
Buffeted by the strong gusts of summer
Scattered across the vastness of the universe
In a whirlwind, gathered again

Love such a soft and evanescent thing,
Fleeting and deadly in form
Melting on a cold tongue of desire
Honing invariably to the nesting place
A place of beauty and enchanting sighs
Of warmth, pervasive and all-consuming
That takes hold of the heart and squeezes
Love with such a gentle caress,
It is so soft like a feather.

Cascading torrent of hormones, sinuous
Ignite a flame where emotion and thought collide
Sending Hiroshima tremors of want of need
That brooks no containment from sinew or bone
In a plume loves' ashes disperse
Like mist caught in a whirlwind
Tossed and scattered about
To settle again once the storm abates

Love gathers again in a whirlwind.
Love is an unending storm
Violent and calm
Tempestuous
It is delightful!

RUNESU CHAZVEMBA

LOVES' ARROW

Oh, cupid, the leveller of all human fields
Cupid, indiscriminate cupid, warm-hearted
Friend to all, lords and commoners
The golden, sinewy arrow of love
Shoots out so fast with the speed of light
And invariably hits its mark,
The centre of the heart is what it aims for
Invariably and without fail, journeys to connect,
With the swiftness of lightning,
Hearts are joined in surprising circumstances
It travels to transform the recipient
Oh, cupid, just as swift in coming
It is also swift-winged in departure
Unless one seizes it and lets it mend
Melting and bonding with one's heart
Bridge the chasm of individuality and binds.
Two entities from far apart meet as one,
Love's arrow sutures and enjoins!

LOVE GONE

There were butterflies of love
In my heart and I felt them
Fluttering softly with their wings
Hovering above the lotus of the heart
Like a mockingbird's wings aflutter,
Beak long and sharp, pecking and
pecking.
For that, nectar in the flower bud is
found.

I knew I loved you
Without cause or reason,
I just loved you.

But your cold, cold responses
To my outstretched endearment
Shrivelled the heart

The frosty responses,
Have had those butterflies in flight.

Spurned, they flew away
To live out their short lives
And perish in the distance
Love,
Sweet love,
Gone.

LOVELY GIRL

Oh, lovely girl
With all my heart, I adore you
Cast in the abyss, I would be without your love
I stretch out my hand in friendship and love
Let our fingers reach out and touch
And entangle in play and rub playfully
Come closer and let us embrace,
That our hearts in tandem beat
Sweet cadence in their duet.

Pristine scents unalloyed by odours
Of artificial fragrances and perfumes
Those that fill the nostrils with rancour
And tickles the nose, exciting a sneeze
You have your natural scent pristine
Fresh, untainted by the odorous stench,
the glamorous modern world bestows.

RUNESU CHAZVEMBA

The purity of your being allures
My gaze was caught in the luminescence of your beauty
Like a rodent in the headlights caught
I stand mesmerized by your beauty nonpareil
Oh, this is an enchanted entrapment
In your embrace, I am shackled
I will not squirm nor ask for quarter
I am gladdened by the power you wield
In the fluttering of your eyelashes
And your soft sigh of contentment.

The emerald green of your eyes
A deep oasis of feeling and innocence
I thirst for the water from the infinite depths
Of that deep pool where consummate love resides
The whole world is a barren desert,
Without your purity of being
Lovely girl, I give my all to you.

RUNESU CHAZVEMBA

FILIAL LOVE

Your entreaties were wise and true
It was folly on my part
That I did not take heed
That I should cleave to the tried and tested
Instead, I wandered off into the wilderness
On a wild goose chase,
most ill-informed.
Look how my compass is broken,
With naught to mend.

What had passed for nagging?
The warm hug of the gravitational force
In retrospect was the greatest of sisterly love
I spurned it out of a sense of adventure
Heedless, I drifted too close to the sun
Oh, look how my pants are on fire
Jeer out if you may, for I deserve it.
This sack, this cloak of ignominy I adorn.

Without a whimper of complaint
Or a moan for mercy
Like the proverbial lamb
In absolute silence to the slaughter led
Oh, sisterly love without bounds
Stretch out a hand and pull me out
From this quagmire, most vile.

Your love is the very earth I stand on,
Stable and unmoved, a firm ground.
I could not spurn it long
Despite the allure of space
The glowing lights of the firmament
Forever taunting me with their brilliance
I sought to hitch myself to the star Sirius,
To behold everyone beneath the starry heavens
In one drooping gaze.

A TORRENT

Glossy-haired Indian beauty,
Garbed in a glossy black lace and bodice
Demurring and firm-breasted beauty,
Petite treasure with soft, voluptuous lips
In a soft made bed in intertwine set

The dame is a fresh oasis,
Upon a chaste desert.

A storm with fury from the North hails
With thunderstorm and grit, the ground trembles
All senses in a torrent swept away
The cactus fronds glisten in the storm
Great heat from the South approaches.
At the equator, a swirling and spinning
clang.

Bond heaven and earth,
Established in a tenacious grip.
In the crown of heaven,
a growl and a moan,
While the Earth is in supplication
Whimpers and trembles.

All universe is enshrouded in a tempestuous wind
Then heaven, with a resounding shudder, quietens
In all the stillness of everything,
Heat streams out
Earth is swamped
And heaven soars.

A CHASM OF LOVE

A deep yearning into a chasm turned
Such a deep need into the abyss tossed
The whirling and churning in the heart stirred,
But what enchantment led into this precipice,
Down the abyss head over heels tossed?

Oh, if you love me
Why won't you stretch out your arms?
And embrace me?
The oceans I make to move
Their waves have a rhythmic sound to serenade
For eons, these serenades I have performed
However, nothing from you I got
Barren, cold, and windswept, I am
Oh, but for a dollop of your love
Life in my veins courses
Love me, Earth, love me
Or into the dark void I am
consumed,
And dashed to oblivion,
I am the moon!

RUNESU CHAZVEMBA

A COMPASSIONATE SWORD

The midwife hoists the rapier high
Gingerly and tenderly severs the umbilical cord
Such an act of love without bounds is shown
Cast adrift in an act of love to live free
A newborn being introduced into the world
By the rapier or sword, into the world brought
It is but an act of love, not hate,
That the rapier is raised

Blooded and glistening in the moonlight,
The rapier shines with mystery,
It is not a sword of hate but of love.
The midwife smiles,
In the fading moonlight light teeth flash,
Bright and white, toothy smile of victory
She sighs, a sigh of contentment and love unbridled.

The coming into existence of a newborn
Comes with agonies of birth, torturous and bloody
Such an act of love
To bring a life form into being.
Under the grime of caking blood oozes life,
And in life the shroud of love
Hangs heavy and soothing.

Love's sword gives life and nurtures life.
Oh, such a compassionate sword!

A LOVE POEM?

The love poem was not just a poem
It was my heart unfurled
Pulsing out of my chest cavity
Oh, you heartless wretch, what did you do with it?
Crumpled it and punched it back in
Now it pulses in a missed, skipped cadence
All innocence of form and beauty lost
Tossed upon the desolate shore,
Of a forbidding sea,
Turgid and briny sea devoid of fish
Or any living creature that roams the
seas.

A gaze across the precipice of a crumbling world
The demurring stares of Venus
Caught in the magnetic embrace of the sun,
Whose love so intense it singes.

Is the fire of heaven love? Mercury
withers in the agonies of love, Venus
resolute smoulders!

The starry sky is a canvas
Upon which a love poem
In a glaring flourish,
Lies emblazoned!

AN ODE TO LOVE

Oh, I fell in love with her voluptuous lips,
Thick and glossy, hanging in fullness.
A moon waxing turgid,
Spilling into fullness of form, shapely
The soft gaze that bathes the soul,
With a divine promise of heaven
A wilting look, eyelashes drooping,
With trappings of the sublime
A blink, a mirror image,
Of the waning and waxing heavenly moon
Soft melting curves that undulate,
Like waves upon the sea
Flowing hair that clings and,
Scatters like enfeebled butterflies
A sweet voice of a summer pregnant
With rains heavy with life
A lilting sound, an echo of a thousand harps,
In a tune melodious to the soul, A twanging
string at the ethereal strumming
By angelic tenderness, slim fingers of the
heart.

The cascading whispers of myriad waterfalls,
Downpouring in unison and with urgency,
A sigh, soothing caress,
The sound of dolphins' therapeutic wailing,
Falling dewdrops upon the desolate lands
Giving succour to all creatures upon the earth
A passion inflamed; a river flooded in a torrent
Irrigating the lowlands nuptial and fertile,
A quickening pulse of rushing streams,
Of desire, that brooks no denial.

Oh, I fell in love with an angel,
Eternal blissful embrace that clings warmly,
Forever soothing the flayed nerves,

 I fell in love with a soul-touching beauty
That cleaves to the essence of being
Love long limbed limbering languidly
On melting snow caps of desire
To coalesce again and again into wholeness
Into fullness realized
Into the full form of truth realized
Life encapsulated into a dewdrop of life

Oh, such a dewdrop of quickening passion
Upon the cacti in a barren desert
A harbinger of life,
Of the beauty of existence
Cast before an eternal canvas
Oh, love, love such a warm embalm
Upon my pulsating heart
Eternally enwrapped
A soft, pleasant caress upon the heart
A sweet rubbing at the sole of the feet
Heart warm and pulsing with an energy ineffable
Swamping of the senses with energies heavy,
The head above the clouds floats,
Detached from the confining limbs,
That tethers one to the mundane realm,
Full of corruption and ennui.

LOVES' TENTACLES

The sweet scent and taste,
Of honey melting on the tongue,
Smooth and soothing,
The flow of milk is cold and creamy
An oily massage,
On jaded nerves of the back,
Bubbling hot shower,
In the searing cold of winter,
Dark shadows of a heavy cloud,
On a hot summer day.

The melting taste of a chocolate ice cream on the
tongue.
A longing and lingering caress,
From the smooth fingers of one's loved one.
The flowing and diaphanous gown of a
newly wedded bride,
Ripples of laughter upon the undulating pool of life.
The enervating taste,
Of immortality in limbs of dreams,
A whimper and sigh of contentment,
On a honeymoon downy bed.

RUNESU CHAZVEMBA

The echo of a familiar sound in a cavernous place.
A billboard proclaiming salvation,
In a desolate plain of despair
A trembling reed in a fast-flowing river,
Bending to the mighty of
a current over-rushing,
An imagination unbridled,
Violent and torrential, A
tempestuous storm,
An inundation of the senses.
Love tentacles enwrapped,
Upon the heart, firm and trembling,
A snare so warm and beautiful,
suffusing all in a glow, enticing.

A LOVE UNWOUND

Thou art sweet-tempered

Compared to the woman who bore Infamy
Veiled from prying tongues that wag,
Spewing venom to defile the whole village
With tales of salacious murmurs abroad.

Of a similar frailty,
One might hasten to say you two possess
Their resolve fails them dismally,
At the heavy thought,
Of asking your hand in friendship,
Yet every iota of men trembles,
I want to join you.

A femme fatale nonpareil Akin
to a bitch in heat.
Pheromones profusion,
To entice the whole neighbourhood,
Limbs led by the nose!

A PEARLY LOVE

She had such a lovely smile once, didn't she?
The lady fortune loves, you loved me,
And favoured me with your beautiful smile
A precious smile so lovely that it lit your face
And lured me into that broad smile
too, A bright, shiny face, a mirror
glazed
To reflect the face of heaven itself.
Sparkling white teeth that shone bright
In the darkest of night, like light bulbs
Lights of magic and beauty overflowing,
Filling the world with soft, sweet energy.

Now her smile is gone!
Taken by the corrosive nature
Of time unwinding.

The once sparkling teeth have fallen out.
Only an empty maw without shine!
An ugly, scary cavern is all that remains,
Bereft of beauty and sparkle
Time, cruel time, the thief of beauty
And sparkle in nature is found,
It robs the living of the sparkle of life
And the beauty in nature is bountiful,
The beauty of the face wiped clean,
And the smile burnt out.
In there somewhere, my beautiful lady fortune,
Love reposes to reawaken,
In a future distant when time tamed,
Sneaks in on none, to snuff out the light of love.

IN THE THROES OF LOVE

The heart in enticement expands
Filling the infinity void with meaning
With a sweet, pungent scent of lavender in spring
Love, a magnificent ball, with alluring magnetic qualities
It flows from the pulsing heart
Spreading to the extremities
A pleasant heat suffuses the body
With a nerve-tingling sensation
The emotions commingling with thought
To conjure an electric field, A warm
and intoxicating, heady taste
Of nirvana experienced.

A soothing, gratifying pleasure upon the nerves,
Flaring without cessation
Basking one in the full glow of the light
Of summer at perihelion
A million butterflies, nectar satiated,
Making a dash for heaven, in the throes of love,
A writhing, sinuous dance ensues.
A tidal wave of blood surges
Through the veins at full speed.
Love-filled and pulsing with life, enchanted
The mind and the senses in tandem rage
Their merging is a symphony of beauty carved
A world with boundless promise and hope emerges
In the throes of love and the world is shaped in
designs pleasant to behold.

RUNESU CHAZVEMBA

THE AFFINITIES

The spheres whirl about each other in their orbit
By their motions, a symphony of sound was made
Inexorably in their orbit they whirl,
Whirl on and on, whispering sweet tunes
to each other as they go.

At the subliminal level, all are bound to each other
By energies invisible to the human eye,
All are held in place enrapt,
Friends, companions in the vast cosmos above.

And below in human affairs are bound in friendships
And there are the humans who prance upon the earth
Affinities that to the human eye are invisible exist; of love of
humanity for humanity fills the world with hope and brightens
The darkness of night with a light so ethereal,
That springs from the heart of all,
All the creatures of the earth are in affinity bound.

RUNESU CHAZVEMBA

LOVE IN STONE

Coiling balm, nectar of the gods
Furled upon itself
And in intertwine with everything else
Huddled in a corner for heat from the cold
A vortex of emotions whirling in a dying dirge
A cold breeze in summer's hot day receding,
A storm tempestuous
But a reprieve in a barren land.

An abundance of fruits and food
In famine-ravaged lands,
A brook winding sinuously down a lush valley
A whisper of excitement in a cold dungeon
A harvest of plenty, a surfeit of food
Love unveiling love availing a precious nugget
Sunk deep into the core of the world, my heart
Resonating with a mind and soul attuned to magic
A magic of existence,
Of a being rising in full form
Love in stone set daring time and oblivion!

CHAPTER THREE

POEMS ON NATURE

All nature is but Art, unknown to thee.
All chance, Direction, which thou canst not see.

-Alexander Pope (1688- 1744) *Essay on Man*

QUIET VALE

Oh, this is a quiet, quiet vale
Upon which I lay my limbs to rest
Oh, this quiet, quiet vale
Where many a drama unfolds
O placid vale undulating
Where a flock of sheep grazes
Bleating peacefully in the day
O verdant vales expansive,
Lush green blade of grass
That undulates in the breeze.
In the gentle breeze of
summer, an enwrapping caress.

To feel the beauty of form,
In the cool of a soft wind,
That blows gently on a hot day
Ruffling the leaves in playfulness
Cooling the skin in a fanned dance
Oh, a quiet vale of beauty
A piece of heaven on earth set
A pristine patch of earth
Where the wind rolls in abandon
Green grasses bend in supplication
A brook placidly glides dauntlessly
Whistling sweet tunes of contentment
Rattling a pebble or two as it flows
A cacophony of nature,
A reminder of the beauty in nature is
found.

THE FRONDS OF SUMMER

The fronds of summer long and wisp fronds,
In the mid-afternoon sun,
Dance about in tune with the
wind.
The fronds of summer,
Wave the day and night away.
Green and lush are the fronds of summer

Bristling in anticipation,
Of the sun and rains intermingled,
On a placid day,
The brooks water leisurely flows,
Reeds by the brook fronds thin and,
Wisp in the brook waters shone
Lush and green are the fronds of summer
The birds perch and flip from frond to frond
In dance with rustling fronds of summer green
In each vein bristling
With the sweet sap of life

PIERIAN SPRING

Deep and sweet-scented are the waters
Of the Pierian Spring,
From these are our thirst quenched.
Sweet-tasting waters
The mental palate to tickle
O those who have imbibed upon these waters
Forever hooked to the sweet waters are they
The muses, with their thirst quenched,
Rises into the air and wax poetic
With such a fluid flow of melody spun
To regale all beings.
Kings and commoners all.
Sparkling clear are the waters,
Of the Pierian Spring
Deep with meaning and,
Enchantments are the springs
Those who have the gift,
Of discernment for subtle essences
Bubble out and weave words of sublime beauty
Smooth flowing with a soft,
Soothing sounds are the waters. To
gaze upon these sinuous waters is
tantalizing to the seat of poetry.

PIGEONS

Pigeons on the roof gathered
A huge flock in a crowd perched
In unison, the flock takes to flight
Wings beating the air and,
Whistling in their flapping
Bluish grey and spangled flock
Into pairs, part and flutter, flutter
One lone pigeon homes in on a
mouse.
Wings stretched upwards.
A V shape formed.
Snatch Mouse flies!

RUNESU CHAZVEMBA

SENTRIES AND GUARDIANS

That the trees and grass
Are naught but bystanders?
In the business of man
It is but an error grievously
For the true nature and purpose
Is but as sentries and guardians
Of the pulsing life.

THE PRICE OF BEAUTY

That he who plants a vineyard by the roadside
Gives tacit consent
To passersby, the fruits partake
That all the beautiful flowers
That in the fields blooms
Bees from everywhere
Would come and take the nectar
It matters not to the flower
That many bees patch
Moreover, the nectar drink
For she lies in supine
At the mercy of the enterprising bees
Brightly petaled flower in the wind waves
A sprite beacon for the honing multitudes of suitors.

Aesthetics is a magnet of grandeur,
And sordidness alike
One must take out the mental wand
And swat the flies of sordidness,
Or beauty is corrupted.

CLOUDS

The lofty ones in the firmaments float

Scudding across the sky, free
An elephant or a horse in the sky made
A warthog glides in a westerly direction
All shapes and forms of clouds in the sky
The burning sun from the gaze of men hid
Heavy pregnant with rain clouds, a shade makes
On the ground, rolling shadows draw
Running, slithering monsters on the ground glide
Scaring enfeebled birds on tree boughs perched
Children in their innocence shadows chase
Clouds, wispy thin clouds higher up in the sky hang
Scudding clouds across the sky move
Destined for other lands
Where succour is needed
A daub of white, greyish colour
On an azure canvas
Drawn with a flourish to excite envy in a Monet,
Clouds in summer in the sky saunter languidly.

RUNESU CHAZVEMBA

LIGHTS IN ALL FORMS

Light of all lights in the firmament hangs
Bright and resplendent in the broad of day
When ashy-fingered dusk approaches
Myriad allies in the skies appear
These lights are many, through wide,
And far distances of space
Twinkle and twinkle an eternal flame,
In the firmament set
Then there is the light of fire,
Which laps and laps and is consumed
Orange and bright, it blazes, dancing in the wind
When the world dons a long, heavy cloak,
Street lights come on, neon and fluorescent,
To wade off the approaching pall of darkness.

RUSTIC SOUNDS

The sweet cooing of a dove

In the suburbia quiet
Conjures up surrealist images
Of the idyllic rustic setting
Here and there, a bird flutters
In flight and playfulness,
A chirping and a shrilly
cry,
Silence split!

RUNESU CHAZVEMBA

VICTORIA FALLS

A thick, white, foamy blanket of water pours
In one continuous stream, it flows
A cascading stream of water in a stream pours

Oh, if there is a clear testimony
Of how nature is a grandmaster
That cleaves the earth and beauty
fashion.
The proof lies deeply embedded
In the Victoria Falls.

That majestic expression of nature,
The cascading mass of white foam
An unending sheet of liquid

In whispering tones, it pours
A mysterious sound of nature
A thunderous whiplash

A remarkable sight,
A mesmerizing, sinuous
dance.
The smoke that thunders!

RUNESU CHAZVEMBA

THE DOME OF HEAVEN

The dome of heaven upon my head rests
Towering in proportions,
Yet featherweight it rests
All that is in heaven upon my head weighs
On a neck steady and shoulders resolute
With the feet spread a shoulder's length apart
The dome of heaven rests upon my head

RAINS

It poured, a heavy cascade of water

This huge heavenly shower pours
With a violence and fury ponderous
Stream upon stream, a downpour
The umbrella unfurled a fragile leaf
Buffeted and pummelled
It strains under the weight
Flapping hectically like a wing of a termite
And in one violent gust snatched out of hand,
Like a discarded napkin in a whirlwind, caught
Pour and pour the relentless torrent pours.

Nature unfurls and opens to the downpour
Tendrils rejoice and wave in supplication,
Sustenance from heaven above sent
In the full glare of the sun, blossom into life.

Ah, rain, the giver of life in tempestuous
times, the sustainer of all
Living things upon the earth.
When sedate and
benevolent,
Succour to all indeed
In a violent temper!
Wrath of nature!

THE MOON HANGS LOW

In an alien world with a vast rocky, patchy
Hurtling down the highway,
In a southerly direction
Looking out the window,
I glance at the most sublime scenery
A silvery ash with dark patches,
Here and there, a sphere of magnificence
Cresting over the horizon,
In all its resplendence and glory
Hanging so near to Earth,
Its companion is almost touching.

SWEPT AWAY

It came frothing with pent-up fury
With a quickening thrust outward
Towards the shore
Turgid and full of wrath, a monstrous wave rose
Inescapable it approaches
In its wake, screams impotent
In one huge wave in an inexorable motion
Swept away and under a ton of water, swamped
In the direction of the shore,
Hurled and drifted to oblivion.

WILTING FRONDS

Wilting fronds droop apathetically
In the full glare of the summer sun
A scorching, blazing torch of heaven
Wilting grass blades are thin and frail
Smouldering death curling in contortions
Life energy from its veins sapped
Drooping in surrender,
Curling into the ground
To merge with
Mother Earth.
A new beginning?

OH, SUNRISE OH SUNSET

Of all the marvels of nature
The sum of all beauties in the land
Oh, sun rise,
Oh, sunset,
The golden hue tinctured
horizon,
In gold, all the clouds are basked.

Oh, gold tinctured gloom
At sunrise, a glorious ascendancy
In sunset, a glorious receding That
leaves a lingering flicker of gold,
glorious dusk has come in full regalia.
The eternal cycle of life,
Birth and death endlessly.

RED WATER LILY

Oh, red water lily
Dazzling in your bloom
Your petals are green and unfurled
Floating across the water
A patch for a toad or a frog
To float and bask in the sun
On a bright noon day,
Oh, glorious water lily,
Green with bright, shiny
leaves
Beauty in nature is encapsulated.

RUNESU CHAZVEMBA

NATURE OF FLOWERS

Flowers in the full glare of the sun bloom
Their petals unfurl, wither, and die
In their core, seeds,
Harbingers of progeny reside
And in the wind are blown away
To seed the world with their flowery nature

Such is the manner of life
The very essence of it,
My rejoinder to your
ruminations: Embrace it.

In each being a seed exists
Awaiting germination
upon the vastness
Of the universe.

THE SIAMESE FIGHTER

Red, purplish aquarium fiend,
In a glassy aquarium ensconced
Vicious fish, friend of mine,
With a mouth in an O shape
When I press my lips to the glass
You press yours too from the other side
To mirror mine, except you are incensed,
And furious with me
For you feel challenged in your aquatic world
In addition, your territorial side flares

The bronze fish,
You have pursued her to exhaustion
I found her struggling to breathe,
Suffocating in tortured lungs
I loved that fish,
She was beautiful and graceful
When she moved, I moved with her
Somehow, you knew of my love for her
You always chased her away from my sight
In passion enraptured,
You fought her to the death
Now the entire aquatic universe is yours
With no one to challenge you.

RUNESU CHAZVEMBA

A FOREST

From a kernel, a whole forest springs
One by one, it sprouts to fill the land
Life expanding to encompass
The whole in its unfurling limbs
Long verdant limbs full of breath, full of life
Each leaf has an image of its progenitor green
Unfurling spurred on by a burst of life
By limbs stretching out to embrace the
heavens, lured by the pulsating heat
Of the serenading sun.

By night, the moon comes into form
Enticing it hangs
A cool breeze waft
Sending the leaves trembling
Oh, life courses through
The veins of all that lives
Trees of the forest do show,
The whole panoply of emotions
Winter cold and forbidding,
To shake the clothes of nature clean
Leaves such a verdant apparel
Wilt and shrivel dry
Barren, stark naked, the trees stand,
Twigs outstretched
Mirroring the roots
In the ground-ensconced firm.

A TUFT OF GRASS

A green tuft of grass
Sprouting from the barren soil
Spreading upon the ground a green carpet
Where nothing but a drab soil lay,
Now it teems with life, bountiful life
A patch of ground barren now fecund
Birds of the air a playground in the lawn found

A sprinkle of manure here and there
And it is all set,
For more fecund is the soil made
Plenty and bountiful is the grass that grows
On a hot summer day, when the ground is parched
A sprinkle of water from a hose gives respite
Dewed leaves in the turgid breeze move
Asserting life and celebrating existence
A green tuft clump of grass, a place to sit,
To rest weary limbs and play about.

INSPIRATION IN NATURE FOUND

When the muses seem to have taken flight
A desolate terrain without magic cast
Bereft of the allure of poetry and prose
A life uneventful ensues, insipid, it drags on
Dull without the chirp of brightly plumed birds
Nor the serenading sound
Of a brook over-rushing
Of the gentle wave of a green blade of grass
Dancing to the eerie sound
Of a song sung by the wind blowing
Oh, nature, bountiful nature,
The restorer of dreams
Contact with you,
A resurgence of creativity ensues
A burst of life,
Bounding with energy and full of promise
The muse's harp hoisted a traipse across the
mind.
Sweet tunes in the veins flow again,
Poetry and prose flow.

RUNESU CHAZVEMBA

A DAY IN SUMMER

Birds chirp shrilly in celebration
It is a beautiful morning, unwinding
The skies hang clear and blue
The air is fresh and crisp, pregnant with life
The fogginess of yesterday, a mere scent fading
That merely clings to the air and ground
Trees and flower plants pleasantly flower
Insects such as bees and flies buzz and gather
Collecting nectar at will
For a greater purpose ahead
Leaves green and lush in the breeze move
A gentle warmth envelops the day
A serene air permeates the area
The mind limbering draws beautiful images
Oh summer, sweet summer, A
gentle cloth I adorn.

THE SOUND OF RAIN

Oh, the sweet melody of falling rains
The drumming sound of raindrops on the pavement
Fluttering sound of rainwater falling on leaves
The beating, pummelling echo
Of rain down a gutter
A reflection of the sky,
In water gathered in a puddle
The dripping of rainwater off the eaves
An ambrosia smell of rain
Filling the air with wonder
The cool, wrapping, enveloping nature,
Of air rain rain-cooled wafts
Drip, a drip, and incessant chant,
Of maddened rains falling
A metronomic grating,
Upon the nerves seeming unending
Conjuring eerie visions,
Of the Chinese water torture
To other ears, a melodious tune it seems,
A tune written up high in the clouds.

RUNESU CHAZVEMBA

PIGEONS' COURTSHIP

Pigeons on a roof ledge
Preen themselves in the sun,
Beneath a bright sun, mate.
Greyish bluish pigeon on a church steeple perched,
It flies off wings beating rhythmically
in the wind.

Pigeons on a roof ledge
Bills meet in a kiss and courtship ritual
And the male circles and,
Perches itself on the back of the female
Wings stretched out in the air, fluttering
As the rear wing in mating flutters up and down.

In the aftermath of their aviary dance
They sit side to side and preen
Facing the sun and
Then turn their backs on each other,
As though ashamed of their deeds, just
A while back.

They preen themselves
Under the wings and on their bellies
Bills connect, and the female almost supplicating crouches
down on its belly
The male hops on her back and
Mates with her again
Rear wing fluttering in the wind

Pigeons in love are paired from birth.
Such constancy is admirable.

RUNESU CHAZVEMBA

THE POWER OF THE INVISIBLE

It is the invisible
It is the insubstantial
That drives the world
It is the invisible upon which
All that unfolds hinges
on the wind, so invisible
yet, do you not feel it?
The tug and the push of its force
When we jump, don't we always come down?
What power invisible control this?

THE FRONDS OF SUMMER

The fronds of summer long and wispy fronds
In the mid-afternoon sun, dance about
In tune with the wind
The fronds of summer wave
The day and night away
Green and lush are the fronds of summer
Bristling in anticipation
Of the sun and rain intermingled
On a placid day, the water of the brook
Leisurely flow
Reeds by the brook fronds thin, and
Wispy in the brook waters show.

AUTUMN BREEZE

Blows with a tempered fury
Sere leaves litter the ground
Trees divested of the cloak of leaves
In the wind, sway no more
In their arrant nakedness stand
Evocative of prurient yearnings
All boughs exposed to lewd eyes
Autumn wind raises a storm of dust
In the eye to cast a cloud of sand
Sultry baneful autumnal winds
To blast a path in nature
To lay barren the terrain about.

PARTING WORLDS

Oh, parting, such sweet sorrowing parting
The familiarity of scenery cleaves to one
The bond and unity with the building
Closeness with the shrubbery
And a cobbled pathway
The too familiar odours of sweat and aromas
The stench of cigarette smoke on the walls caught
The endearing smiles
Of friends and acquaintances
The camaraderie engendered in close quarters
Oh, parting, such sweet sorrowing parting
Of one season from the other,
Each to walk its part for a while,
Then in its turn to part.

RUNESU CHAZVEMBA

TSUNAMI OF EMOTIONS

It came frothing with pent-up fury
With a quickening thrust outwards
Toward the shore
Turgid and full of wrath
A monstrous wave rose
Inescapable it approaches
In its wake, screams impotent
In one huge wave in an inexorable motion
Swept away and under a ton of water, swamped
In the direction of the shore
Hurled and drifted to oblivion.

Its ire yet unspent
Roiling boiling fury
Onto land it continued
Venting its unbridled angst
Sweeping the ground beneath its wake,
Unrelenting force of nature
An unreasoning monstrosity

This Tsunami of emotions
Rising from the vast sea of feeling!

A FEISTY BREEZE

There is a cool, feisty breeze
That from a westerly direction waft
It blows and blows
With a force and fury of nature
Against the balustrade
Circumscribing the back balcony blows
It whistles pleasantly
Where it meets the railings
And out the back door window
The fronds of the palm tree
In the wind waves and waves
Vigorously with a rustling sound
A giant tree from across the road
Sways demurely in the wind
The multifarious green leaves flutter,
Flutter in the force of the wind
Like the wings of birds in flight
With a glitter and a sheen, the leaves flutter.

THE BROWN FROG

Fat, ugly, venomous frog
Oozing with venom in every pore
Brown fat frog skin mottled
Breathing in incensed vitriol
Sloe-eyed venomous brown frog
Leaping from one lily leaf to another
Leaving a trail of slime behind
And sending a splutter of browned, dirty water
Messing with the black polished shoes of the gentry
The flowing white dresses of the women
A croak in the early hours of the night is eerie
A croak in the early hours of the morning.

WHISPERS OF THE DARK RACE

Whispers of the Dark Race is a multi-faceted tale of Africa, unfolding and unfurling its wings, catching the wind as it goes, and soaring to the heavens fully formed and brightly plumed as she rises. The poems are a ricochet through the sacred hall of ancient times, a time when trees whispered sweet tunes and rocks drummed melodious tunes in the night. It shows men ascending to the highest level attainable. It reveals the mind; the conductor whose indefatigable fingers strum the multiple-stringed guitar of the universe of the mind! It takes you through antiquity to the present and soars forth to the future whose plains are pure and not profaned by negative experiences of a past singed and a present in flames. The book dashes out a mosaic with a flourish and abandon that knows no restraint nor inhibition. On a vast canvas stretching the length and breadth of the globe, steered by the compass of what is proper. A piece from Europe spun, a flake from Asia, melting on the tongue, hot and spicy. It seeks to paint the bright glare of the Americas' smouldering ancient ruins. In all this, Africa reposes, the centre piece of it all, the hinge upon which everything revolves, spinning a web of poetry and prose.

ABOUT THE AUTHOR

Runesu Chazvemba is an educator, philosopher, researcher, therapist, and a prolific writer loaded with tales that elevate man to heights never seen or experienced before; sci-fi, poetry, adventures, plays, and all forms of creative writing. He enjoys spinning enticing stories. His quest is to carve a new world in words and regale the world with the beauty of form and structure, transport his readers to the distant realms far within the cranial and together to partake in the game of life in universes of collective creation. He is a dreamer and creator of worlds. He ushers in all those who would like to be co-creators with him, not to hesitate but to reach forth for the abode of poetry and prose. An adventure awaits right at the periphery of your mind, ready to bedazzle you with a soul-tingling joy.

GLOSSARY

[1] **Ptah**: an ancient Egyptian deity, god of craftsmen and architects.

[1] **Ankh**: an object design resembling a cross but having a loop instead of the top arm, used in ancient Egypt as a symbol of life.

[1] **Djeb**: an ancient Egyptian symbol for stability, which is pillar-like in shape

[1] **Was Sceptre**: an ancient Egyptian symbol of power and dominion, it has a straight shaft, crooked handle in the shape of an animal head, and a forked base.

[1] **Lord Ra**: In ancient Egyptian religion, the god of the sun and creator god.

[1] **Patina**: a crust or film that happens from use or exposure to oxygen.

BOOKS BY THIS AUTHOR

Other Worlds Untold: An Anthology of African Poetry by Runesu Chazvemba

A panoply of poems all in free verse exploring the abstract and enchanting, sublime realm carved in words and drawn with such an abandon and flourish upon the vast canvas of a creative tapestry. The poems beg to be felt, to be perceived through a faculty that cleaves to something ineffable and yet draws upon the effervescent, that deep yearning chasm only the beauty of sound and word can satiate. It is an invitation to tune into the whispers and resonance of that seat of aesthetics. Poetry has form, imagery, and style that find acquaintance with and invite familiarity with a much broader audience. The poems solicit the participation of the reader, where the reader is enticed into and consequently immersed in the sparkling waters of the Pierian Spring and, as one, flows down enchanted brooks and tastes the sweetness of inclusivity where all waters meet in the vast ocean of feeling and being.

Kemet Awakening: African Poetry Resurgence by Runesu Chazvemba

Kemet Awakening is a quintessential symphony cascading from the heart of Africa. Where, for eons, the pulse of the world was tuned, and from which its resonance fills the world with a melody that sustains the world's flora and fauna. If there is a language everlasting, the poetry in this work captures it and gives it form, in that allowing all to see the visions of nirvana of Valhalla, of Jannah, of heaven, all erstwhile preserves of the shaman, the Bodhi, the adept, the spiritually gifted. A dive into that infinite creativity pool whose depths are unfathomable and yet capable of being perceived in their full and colourful regalia! A scintillating read!

The Organ Collectors: And Other Short Stories by Runesu Chazvemba, Natalie Chazvemba, and Mirek Fajer

The Organ Collectors and Other Short Stories is a collection of fictional stories (and a single nostalgic piece) from a diverse base of authors who came together as a family to express their creativity. Be prepared for a unique experience with every story. The story, which lends its name to this book's title, is written by Runesu Chazvemba and centres on a man who sought out an eastern religious experience, lured by the promise of enlightenment. He attends a ceremony only to discover that he is missing a kidney. The story takes us into the underworld of the organ transplant Black Market, where the most cunning schemes are unravelled.

Be prepared for an emotional response and your thoughts to be provoked!

Excerpts from 'The Organ Collectors: And Other Short Stories'

"I was born in the year 800. I was a beautiful child. At least my mother said so. Our home was in the valley of the Perun's mountains, and stormy outbursts of his power left strong impressions upon my young mind. I loved it thoroughly. For all its beauty, the land was rather harsh on our farming family, as mountains usually are. We were a family of five people, that is my father, mother, older brother and sister, and of course, me, Draga." *Byzance*

"Gracie was six when she was transported back in time. She became used to the conditions in the early 1900s to the extent that her past, the present, and the future were all dream-like. She had once tried to explain that she wanted pizza for lunch. This was met by startled confusion as pizza had not become a common lunch item in Durban at the time." *The Vanishing*

"The amniotic fluid, like, arrests decay, and the incenses take care of the smell, perfuming the putrefaction out of the corpse. Three weeks in the resurrection tank restores the body to almost its pristine state. The body would, however, be devoid of the quality of animation, that one quality which distinguishes between the cadaver and the living." *Dr. Melancholia*

.